Edited by
ANDREW ROBERTS
CAROLINE HOMAN
NEIL JOHNSON
and **TOM MILTON**

BREAKING BREAD

❝ They devoted themselves
to the apostles' teaching and to
fellowship, **to the breaking**
of bread and to prayer. **❞**

The Bible Reading Fellowship
15 The Chambers, Vineyard
Abingdon OX14 3FE
brf.org.uk

The Bible Reading Fellowship (BRF) is a Registered Charity (233280)

ISBN 978 0 85746 680 8
First published 2018
Reprinted 2018
10 9 8 7 6 5 4 3 2 1
All rights reserved

Text © individual authors 2018
This edition © The Bible Reading Fellowship 2018
Original design by morsebrowndesign.co.uk & penguinboy.net

Acknowledgements
Unless otherwise acknowledged, scripture quotations from The New Revised Standard
Version of the Bible, Anglicised edition, copyright © 1989, 1995 by the Division of Christian
Education of the National Council of the churches of Christ in the United States of
America. Used by permission. All rights reserved.

Scripture quotations on cover and title page, or marked NIV, are taken from The Holy
Bible, New International Version (Anglicised edition) copyright © 1979, 1984, 2011 by
Biblica. Used by permission of Hodder & Stoughton Publishers, a Hachette UK company.
All rights reserved. 'NIV' is a registered trademark of Biblica. UK trademark number
1448790.

Photographs on pages 39 and 43 copyright © Thinkstock; photograph on page 63
copyright © FreeImages.com/spiz; photographs on pages 4, 11, 19, 29, 31, 35 and 53
copyright © Tom Milton and the Birmingham Methodist Circuit.

Every effort has been made to trace and contact copyright owners for material used in
this resource. We apologise for any inadvertent omissions or errors, and would ask those
concerned to contact us so that full acknowledgement can be made in the future.

A catalogue record for this book is available from the British Library

Printed and bound by CPI Group (UK) Ltd, Croydon CR0 4YY

CONTENTS

Remember the context

This Holy Habit is set in the context of ten Holy Habits, and the ongoing life of your church and community.

> **They devoted themselves** to the apostles' teaching and fellowship, **to the breaking of bread** and the prayers. Awe came upon everyone, because many wonders and signs were being done by the apostles. All who believed were together and had all things in common; they would sell their possessions and goods and distribute the proceeds to all, as any had need. Day by day, as they spent much time together in the temple, they broke bread at home and ate their food with glad and generous hearts, praising God and having the goodwill of all the people. And day by day the Lord added to their number those who were being saved.
>
> ACTS 2:42–47

A prayer for the faithful practice of Holy Habits

This prayer starts with a passage from Romans 5:4–5.

> Endurance produces character, and character produces hope,
>   and hope does not disappoint us…
> Gracious and ever-loving God, we offer our lives to you.
> Help us always to be open to your Spirit in our thoughts
>   and feelings and actions.
> Support us as we seek to learn more about those habits of the Christian life
>   which, as we practise them, will form in us the character of Jesus
>   by establishing us in the way of faith, hope and love.
> Amen

INTRODUCTION

The breaking of bread is a distinctive term of Luke, the author of Acts. He uses it most powerfully when Cleopas and his companion describe how Jesus had been made known to them 'in the breaking of the bread' (Luke 24:35).

It is not clear from Acts 2:42 how Luke is using the term when describing the life of the first Christian communities. Commentators are cagey about its use. Is it describing the act which opened a common Jewish meal? Is it a specific liturgical and sacramental act? C.K. Barrett argues that '"breaking of bread" was not a Jewish term for a meal and in this sense must have been a Christian development' (*Acts 1–14*, T&T Clark, 2004, p. 165), i.e. an embryonic service of Holy Communion. James Dunn is more circumspect, suggesting, 'We may assume that on some occasions at least the meal included a shared commemoration of the last supper but Luke has not gone out of his way to make this plain' (*The Acts of the Apostles*, Epworth, 1996, p. 35). Hans Conzelmann points out that Luke makes no attempt to distinguish between an ordinary meal and the 'Eucharist' and suggests that 'the unity of the two is part of the ideal picture of the earliest church' (*The Acts of the Apostles*, Fortress, 1987, p. 23).

This exploration of **Breaking Bread** works with a broad understanding of the term: one that includes and honours the practice of Holy Communion, but reflects upon **Breaking Bread** in other ways and contexts too – ways that also make Jesus known.

When exploring the specific sacramental act in which bread is broken and wine shared, the term 'Holy Communion' is used most often. Other terms such as the Lord's Supper and the Eucharist are also used when appropriate to represent different perspectives and traditions.

 Resources particularly suitable for children and families

☺ Resources particularly suitable for young people

CH4   Church Hymnary 4 (also known as Hymns of Glory Songs of Praise)
RS   Rejoice and Sing
SoF   Songs of Fellowship 6
StF   Singing the Faith

Reflections

In first developing this resource, the team from the Birmingham Methodist Circuit centred their thinking on the reminder that the early Christians found God in every aspect of life and that they gathered together to share their lives as a community. They made mistakes, they didn't always share and yet they found something so special that they tried to follow Christ's example. So they, like him, took bread, the ordinary and everyday; they gave thanks to God, they broke it, they shared it and they consumed it.

Through **Breaking Bread**, you too are invited to gather and take the everyday; thanking God for it, breaking it, sharing it and eating it. And as you do this, in many varied ways, including sharing Holy Communion with Christ, our prayer is that you will be transformed by God's love and be people energised by the Spirit to play your part in transfiguring your churches, your communities and the world beyond so that God's kingdom may grow on earth as in heaven.

Above all, our prayer is that this habit helps you to deepen your trust, knowing yourself loved by God and challenging you to offer God your love, individually, as a church and as a community, through your living alongside others as a thankful, broken, blessed and sharing people.

Please refer to the notes in the Holy Habits Introductory Guide about considering the needs of those with diabetes, food allergies or intolerances, eating disorders or other restrictions around food and drink.

UNDERSTANDING THE HABIT

WORSHIP RESOURCES

Below are some thoughts and ideas for how you might incorporate this Holy Habit into worship.

Biblical material

Old Testament passages:

- Exodus 16 — Manna is given to the hungry in the wilderness
- 1 Kings 17:8–16 — Elijah and the widow's supply of food
- Jeremiah 16:5–13 — No one will **Break Bread** to offer comfort to those who mourn

Gospel passages:

- Matthew 26:17–30 — The institution of the Lord's Supper
- Mark 14:12–31 — The institution of the Lord's Supper
- Luke 11:1–4 — The Lord's Prayer
- Luke 22:7–23 — The institution of the Lord's Supper
- Luke 24:13–35 — The meal at Emmaus
- Luke 24:36–49 — A meal speaking of brokenness, transformation and tradition
- John 6 — Feeding of 5,000, bread, Jesus and food for life
- John 21:1–19 — Breakfast on the beach

Other New Testament passages:

- Acts 2:42–47 — The breaking of bread
- 1 Corinthians 11:23–26 — The words of institution at the last supper

Suggested hymns and songs

- As we break the bread (RS 439)
- Behold the Lamb (Communion hymn) (SoF 1724) ☺
- Be known to us in breaking bread (RS 441, StF 573)
- Bread of the world (RS 443)
- Come, Host of heaven (StF 680)
- Come, now, you blessed, eat at my table (StF 695)
- Down to earth (**www.fischy.com**)
- Eat this bread, drink this cup (CH4 671, StF 583)
- God beside (**www.fischy.com**)
- Great God, your love has called us here (CH4 484, RS 339, StF 499)
- I come with joy (CH4 656, StF 588)
- Jesus calls us here to meet him (RS 510, StF 28)
- Jesus the Lord said: 'I am the Bread' (RS 199, StF 252)
- Lord, we come to ask your healing (StF 652)
- Lord, we have come at your own invitation (CH4 638, StF 595)
- Our hunger cries from plenty (RS 341)
- Put peace into each other's hands (CH4 659, RS 635, StF 712)
- Reap me the earth (RS 437)
- Remembrance (Communion song) (SoF 2471) ☺
- Strengthen for service (RS 461)
- The church is like a table (RS 480)
- The table (SoF 2915) ☺

Introduction to the theme 👪

Place a table at the front or centre of your worshipping space. Dress the table nicely with a cloth and a centrepiece (perhaps a cross, a flower or a bowl of water and some pebbles). Place a large plate upon the table with a range of pieces of bread upon it. Remember to include at least one piece of gluten-free bread, taking care to place this in a way that prevents it touching the other bread.

If time permits, you could meet before the service to bake some of the bread that you place on the table. If you have or can borrow bread makers, then have one or two of these baking bread as you meet so that the fragrance adds to the occasion.

Invite a group of people to come and sit around the table – making this group as diverse as possible. Sit among them and facilitate a conversation about bread. This is a conversation you want the congregation to listen in to and get involved with. Start by asking people what their favourite type of bread is. Invite those at the table to sample some of the bread on the table. Ask them to say which is their favourite and why. Then ask people to think and share times and places when they **Break Bread**. Encourage a range of answers: e.g. when I am eating my lunch at work, when we share Holy Communion, when I volunteer at the day-care centre. Point out the range of contexts in which we break bread and how the Christian practice of **Breaking Bread** began in homes: at the last supper and in the church Luke describes in Acts 2. Sometimes this may have been as part of a meal, sometimes as part of an early form of Holy Communion service. Sometimes both. On all occasions, the breaking of bread would remind people of Jesus and help them to recognise his presence with them.

Invite people to take the bread from the table (either now or at the end of the service) and to do one of two things with it later in the day:

- Break it and share it with a prayer of grace before a meal at home.
- Take it as a gift to someone in need of help or encouragement.

Encourage people to notice how they sensed the presence of Jesus when they shared bread in either of these two ways.

Thoughts for sermon preparation

Luke 24:30–35

> When he was at the table with them, he took bread, blessed and broke it, and gave it to them. Then their eyes were opened, and they recognised him; and he vanished from their sight. They said to each other, 'Were not our hearts burning within us while he was talking to us on the road, while he was opening the scriptures to us?' That same hour they got up and returned to Jerusalem; and they found the eleven and their companions gathered together. They were saying, 'The Lord has risen indeed, and he has appeared to Simon!' Then they told what had happened on the road, and how he had been made known to them in the breaking of the bread.

The term **Breaking Bread** is intriguing. Depending upon whom you speak to and which biblical commentary you consult, a range of understandings emerges. Maybe that's because we each experience God in different ways. Some might be led by intellect through words, and some by emotions through experience. Some could be mystics, finding God in images and symbols, and some activists, finding God in acts of mercy and justice. To add to the complexity, each one of us is probably a mixture of two or even all of these approaches. In light of all this, might there not be scope to approach this Holy Habit with a sense of childlike wonder? If, in **Breaking Bread**, Christ becomes known, is it possible that the reflections and sermons we share in exploring this Holy Habit might seek to provide a glimmer of 'realness' which seeks to engage with our own realness and the realness of the people we serve?

The Velveteen Rabbit is a classic children's story book. It tells the tale of a stuffed rabbit who is on a mission to become real, or known, through the love of his owner. Using this little story as inspiration, is it possible that, through the love of the one who owns us, we might become real enough to allow 'the one' to be known through us as we break open the word? If so, how might this story help us to explore that through all of our senses?

In the story, the little boy holds the velveteen rabbit so lovingly and persistently that eventually all his fur is loved off. Amazingly, the rabbit then somehow becomes real through his brokenness. After the resurrection, when Jesus sat at the table with the disciples and later when he appeared to them in the upper room he was within touching distance, still bearing the scars of a real and incarnate love, and suddenly in that brokenness he became very real.

Are there moments of realness we could highlight in our preaching that might reveal the resurrected Christ in the ordinariness of our brokenness? Moments like: the breaking of bread; the comforting hug of a friend; a look of love or a smile from a stranger; the taste of shared meals or the bitter saltiness of tears shed; the beauty of intense silence when only silence will suffice? Can we be brave enough to share how God is real in our lives and listen with humility to how God is present in the lives of others?

In all things be real.

For further suggestions, see StF 568–602 (Holy Communion) and StF 749–790 (Liturgical Settings) or search Singing the Faith Plus (**www.singingthefaithplus.org. uk**).

Prayers

Liturgy for Holy Communion

This liturgy was produced by the Birmingham Methodist Circuit when they developed the first Holy Habits programme. You may wish to adapt it to fit your context, or to develop a liturgy that is birthed in your location and culture. Could the act of writing a liturgy help a home group or youth group explore the group's experience and understanding of Holy Communion? If you do develop your own material, please see the notes in the 'Going further with the habit' section that introduce and explain the key elements of a liturgy for Holy Communion.

You might consider whether you could offer this with all ages together. Perhaps some could bake bread or dampers and others prepare the table, or make crafts during worship which could be presented as part of the offering.

Welcome and prayer of approach

> Lord God, we offer you our city, as a community which desires to **Break Bread** together as brothers and sisters, united in and by your love. Be present with us we pray, here in this place and throughout our streets, our waterways and our parks. Call us to your table, to feast as one body.

Prayers of praise and thanksgiving

> For the love you have for all your children,
> abundant and unending,
> eternal and unchanging
> **God we give you praise and thanks.**
>
> For the beauty and diversity of your creation,
> glorious and surprising,
> reminding us of your power and creativity
> **God we give you praise and thanks.**
>
> For the people who surround us,
> teaching us of your love and showing us something of your nature,
> who enrich us and our communities
> **God we give you praise and thanks.**

Prayers of confession

We seek to be a community where all may eat and sleep in peace and safety,
but we know that we, and our city, often fall short.

Forgive us, most merciful God,
when we do not love our city, others, ourselves and you,
as you have commanded.
Christ have mercy, Christ forgive us.

Forgive us when we do not offer hospitality and a welcome,
when we do not provide a seat at the table for those who have none.
Christ have mercy, Christ forgive us.

By your grace, change our hearts to be more like yours,
always open, always ready and always loving.
Christ have mercy, Christ forgive us.

Our God always waits for us to turn again to him
and offers us his love and forgiveness,
freely and without reserve.
We are welcome at his table.

Readings and sermon to be inserted here.

Prayers of intercession

God who is just and righteous,
be with those in our city who are oppressed.
Those who live in financial insecurity,
those who are homeless,
those who are told they are illegal,
those whose pain is private, hidden in violence and neglect.
We ask for your peace to surround them,
your love to comfort them,
and your light to give them hope.

God who is kind and generous,
be with those who give of their time and energy to build our communities
and nourish our common life.
Strengthen and embolden them to build your kingdom,

equip them, and us, to serve your children,
give them rest,
and encourage them in their doing and their being.

God who is wise and powerful,
be with our leaders and in their decisions.
May they be guided by justice and selflessness
rather than greed and a desire for influence,
may they seek what is best for your people in love and compassion.
Give them the strength to be courageous when doing what is right
in the face of opposition.

God of justice
God of righteousness
God of kindness
God of generosity
God of wisdom
God of power
Hear our prayer as we lift our city to you.

Amen

The table is prepared and the offerings are placed on it:

Most holy and most present God, we offer you our gifts of time and talents,
personalities and money. We offer you our homes and our city. We offer you
bread and wine all for transformation through your grace and love.
Amen

The great prayer of thanksgiving is made:

God is with us.
Thanks be to God.

God is far beyond us.
Thanks be to God.

We offer God our worship.
We offer God our love.

Glorious God, you breathed hope and the world was created.
You spoke and creatures lived.

You love all that you have made,
You love our city, our community, our church, ourselves.

Though we ignore you, doubt you, treat your creation cruelly; you always love, you always hope, you always prompt. Abraham and Sarah, Ruth and Naomi, David and Isaiah all speak of your surprising, healing presence.

When the time was right, you sent your Son and our Saviour Jesus to love us, to live in country and in city, completely human and completely divine, to die for us and to show in resurrection glory that your love is stronger than hatred, your life is mightier than even death itself.

So with people throughout time and with the choirs of heaven we share words of hope and praise:

Holy, holy, holy Lord,
God of power and might,
Heaven and earth are full of your glory.
Hosanna in the highest.
Blessed is he who comes in the name of the Lord.
Hosanna in the highest.

Creative, caring God, we can only begin to imagine how, on that night surrounded by fear, violence and betrayal, our life-giving Jesus took the day's bread, thanked you for it, broke it, gave it to his companions and said, 'Take, eat. This is my body given for you. Do this to remember me.'

After supper, he took the cup, thanked you again and gave it to all saying, 'This cup is the new covenant of my blood, shed for you and for everyone for the forgiveness of sin. Do this to remember me.'

We remember that Jesus gave his life for us and for the whole world. We believe the story of the resurrection and we long to share Christ's life:

Christ has died. Christ is alive. Christ will come again.

Send your Holy Spirit that these gifts of bread and wine may be, for us, Christ's saving body and blood. May this same Spirit live in us that we might cherish and share Christ's sacrificial and healing love with all. So may we be united with all your people in our city, across the world and in heaven. May we love and honour you for ever, through Jesus your Son in the unity of the Holy Spirit.
Amen

Our church and our city are diverse, so in whatever form or language comes from our heart we say:

Our Father in heaven,
hallowed be your name,
your kingdom come,
your will be done,
on earth as in heaven.
Give us today our daily bread.
Forgive us our sins
as we forgive those who sin against us.
Save us from the time of trial
and deliver us from evil.
For the kingdom, the power,
and the glory are yours
now and for ever.
Amen

The bread we break is a sharing in the body of Christ.
Christ is the living bread.

The wine we drink is a sharing in the blood of Christ.
Christ is the true vine.

Those administering receive either now or after all have received.

The table belongs not to us but to God. Christ welcomes all. So let us share together…

Words of administration may be as custom or with the words: The body of Christ given for you, The blood of Christ shed for you.

After all have received:

Let us pray together:
Generous God, you are with us and have offered us a taste of heaven and its banquet. This is your gift for all people. As we have received, so help us to give.
Amen

Christ has shared his peace with us. Let us share it first with one another and then with those we will meet far beyond this place:

The peace of Christ be with you.
And also with you.

The peace is shared.

Blessing

God the Creator of life in countryside and city,
God the Giver of resurrection life,
God the Spirit of love and life,
God bless us and through us may our homes, our city, our world
be blessed in the name of God; Father, Son and Spirit.
Amen

Go in peace to love and serve God.
In the name of Christ
Amen

A simple order of service for an Agape or Love Feast

Love Feasts were part of the early life of the Methodist movement, an act of **Worship** and **Fellowship** that has been more widely engaged with again in recent years. There is no set liturgy for a Love Feast, so there is freedom to adapt this idea to whatever setting you choose. It could lend itself to all-age worship or Messy Church events, for example. The basic idea is to share food, song, prayer and story around a common loving-cup of grace. The following liturgy is offered for you to use in full or adapt appropriately.

Opening song
Jesus calls us here to meet him (StF 28)

Welcome
Whether today is your first time worshipping with us or whether this is your home of worship, a very warm welcome.

In today's service we will share a Love Feast together, which embraces many of our Holy Habits, including **Eating Together** and **Prayer**. Traditionally, a Love Feast celebrates a sense of common purpose or community and the joy of praising God in song. Testimony and story are shared with an emphasis on our experience of God. We share cake and water in anticipation of the heavenly banquet 'prepared for all'. We pray for one another before remembering others in our offering. Then we journey out to continue our worship and service in the world.

Bible reading of choice

Song
Come, and let us sweetly join (StF 646)

Gospel reading

Hymn

Short prayer of grace

Share food and testimony
Allow a set time for small groups to share what God has done in their lives as water and cake is enjoyed. This can be a moving and fruitful way of encouraging others to consider the call of Jesus and hence of **Making More Disciples**.

Prayer
Prayers are spoken in small groups and rounded up by whoever is leading worship.

Hymn

Blessing

Dismissal
As we leave, we are invited to make a contribution to an offering which will be given for (add charity of choice). This was an original feature of all Methodist Love Feasts.

Different ways of praying

Prayer of praise and adoration

Display pictures of bread in different places around the worship space or use images on PowerPoint.

Invite the congregation to pray in silence with eyes open and give thanks.

Reassure them that if the images cause their minds to wander, reminding them of people, places or events, that's okay and is part of their prayer.

Meditation

Get a selection of rolls from a bakery or supermarket that sells rolls individually.

Read the feeding of the 5,000 several times (Matthew 14:13–21, Mark 6:30–44, Luke 9:10–17 or John 6:1–14). Alternatively, read it once and display the words on the screen or invite the congregation to read from their pew Bibles.

As the words are read, pass the rolls around the congregation and invite people to take a chunk of bread to help them meditate on the scripture.

Remind them to listen to God.

After about ten minutes, encourage a time of sharing in small groups or all together, depending on the size of your congregation.

Give people permission to sit with their own thoughts if they do not wish to share.

Three plates

Set up three plates, either as a centrepiece for a congregation or as a prayer station.

On the first plate place a complete bread roll, on the second place some large crumbs or leftovers, and leave the third plate empty.

Either have the following prayers printed on three cards, one next to each plate, or read them out to the congregation as they focus on each of the three plates.

Plate 1

Bread nourishes us!
Let us bring before God the times when we have felt nourished...

(*Silence*)

For all that we have been given
For times of fulfilment
For times of satisfaction
For times of abundance
We thank you, God!

Plate 2

Only the crumbs were left!
Let us bring before God those times when we have seen only leftovers and crumbs...

(*Silence*)

For times when abundance and plenty is only a memory
For times when it seems impossible not to covet what others have
For times when there is barely enough to sustain
God, help us to recognise and use what we do have.

Plate 3

The cupboard was bare!
Let us bring before God those times when we or others have had nothing...

(*Silence*)

For the times when there is nothing to give and nothing to take
For the times we are overlooked
For the times we overlook others
God, give us what we need

Jesus encouraged his disciples to trust God to give them their daily bread, so let us pray as Jesus taught us:

Our Father...

GROUP MATERIAL AND ACTIVITIES

Some of these small group materials are traditional Bible studies, some are more diverse session plans and others are short activities, reflections and discussions. Please choose materials appropriate to whatever group you are working with.

Breaking bread

Readings from Matthew, Mark, Luke and others

'The breaking of the bread': the Greek original of the New Testament only has the exact equivalent of this phrase in two places. Look up Luke 24:35 and Acts 2:42. Familiarise yourselves with the passage in which each verse occurs, and then discuss or ponder the question of whether or not the phrase suggests something special is being referred to, and whether it refers to the same thing in both passages. Hold your answers to come back to.

Now look at a selection of the following verses, again observing the story in which they occur. If you are in a group, each person could find one and share it with the others; you need not look them all up, depending on time available. Note or discuss what your passages have in common, and where they differ. Do this before reading the notes below.

- Matthew 14:19; 15:36; 26:26
- Mark 6:41; 8:6, 19; 14:22
- Luke 9:16; 22:19; 24:30

In these passages, it is always Jesus who gives thanks or blesses the bread, then breaks and shares it. It seems an action characteristic of him. Does that shed light on the phrase in one of those opening verses, Luke 24:35? Remember Jesus is recognised by this action, as if it is something special to him, not just the blessing any Jew would offer before a meal. The same actions occur in all these passages; however, in the 'feeding of the multitude' stories it appears that everyone is included – food is showered on people in abundance – whereas in the last supper narratives Jesus shares just with his intimate group of disciples. The feeding stories implicitly (explicitly in John 6) associate what happened with God's gift of manna in the desert at the time of Israel's exodus from Egypt; whereas the last supper narratives suggest that these actions are to do with Jesus' body soon to be broken on the cross. What difference do you think that makes? Is **Breaking Bread** a sign of the kingdom, or is it a memorial of Christ's death?

All of these Gospels associate the last supper with Passover. In John's Gospel, the association with Passover is made in a different way: Jesus dies when the Passover lambs are being sacrificed in the temple in preparation for the Passover meal (John 18:28; 19:14), and a scriptural text about the Passover lamb is applied to Jesus' dead body – 'none of his bones shall be broken' (John 19:36; cf. Exodus. 12:46; Numbers. 9:11). Paul wrote 'Christ, our Passover lamb, has been sacrificed' (1 Corinthians 5:7, NIV). So the breaking of the bread points to the story about Israel being freed from slavery in Egypt as a model for understanding how Christ dies to free humankind from the tyranny of sin and death – the blood on the doorposts averts the angel of death, and the meat/bread strengthens for the journey. Jewish teachers around the time of Jesus associated with Passover God's gift of manna on the journey through the desert, and John's Gospel brings all these themes together in chapter 6, his feeding story. So the answer to the question about whether the breaking of the bread is a sign of the kingdom or a memorial of Christ's death may be not 'either-or' but 'both-and'.

Now turn to another selection of verses and study them in the same way.

- Acts 2:46; 20:7, 11; 27:35
- 1 Corinthians 10:16; 11:24

In all these passages, **Breaking Bread** has apparently become characteristic of the Christian community, as before it was characteristic of Jesus; but is it always special or often just sharing meals? Three things to consider:

- **Prayer** is nearly always associated with **Breaking Bread**.
- Often the action imitates those characteristic actions of Jesus.
- In Paul's letter, **Breaking Bread** is associated with the last supper, whereas that is never entirely clear in Acts. However, in Acts 2:42 (the other of our opening verses), the phrase 'the breaking of the bread' sounds like a kind of 'technical term' – rather like someone now speaking of 'the Communion' or 'the Eucharist'.

In the light of these scriptures and your thoughts or discussions, explore these questions:

1 Should blessing, breaking and sharing bread be 'special' or ordinary? Should this be a 'holy habit' whenever we meet together?
2 Should **Breaking Bread** be exclusively reserved for the Christian community, or did Jesus give the bread to the disciples to distribute to everybody?
3 What might all this mean for:
   ○ our relationship with food in general?
   ○ our understanding of the sacrament?

John Wesley wrote a sermon on 'The Duty of Constant Communion'. You could finish by reading the following extracts:

> The first reason why it is the duty of every Christian [to receive the Lord's Supper as often as he can] is because it is a plain command of Christ. That this is his command appears from the words of the text – 'Do this in remembrance of me'… They are… his dying words to all his followers.

> A second reason why every Christian should do this as often as he can is because the benefits of doing it are so great to all that do it in obedience to him – namely, the forgiveness of our past sins and the present strengthening and refreshing of our souls…

> The grace of God given herein confirms to us the pardon of our sins by enabling us to leave them. As our bodies are strengthened by bread and wine, so are our souls by these tokens of the body and blood of Christ. This is the food of our souls: this gives strength to perform our duty and leads us on to perfection…

> In order to understand the nature of the Lord's Supper, it would be useful carefully to read over those passages in the Gospel, and in the first epistle to the Corinthians, which speak of the institution of it. Hence we learn that the design of this sacrament is the continual remembrance of the death of Christ, by eating bread and drinking wine, which are the outward signs of the inward grace – the body and blood of Christ.

For further discussion

If you want to explore this further, you can follow discussions of 'The Duty of Constant Communion', in volume 2, issue 1 of Wesley House's *Holiness* journal (**www.wesley. cam.ac.uk/holiness**).

The last supper 👪 ☺

Mark 14:12–31

Begin by asking people if they have special family traditions or foods that they eat at special times. What makes the meals special? Are there things that they don't enjoy about them?

We are going to hear about a very special meal that Jesus had with his disciples just before he died. Ask people if they know about the Passover celebrations and the significance of unleavened bread. If they don't, give a brief explanation. You could also add that the upper room was often used by teachers or guests of the house.

Give people characters from the story to focus on before the story is read. They could be one of the disciples who went ahead, Jesus, Peter or Judas. Read the story from Mark's Gospel (the Dramatised Bible version is good) or the story from the DLTK website (**www.dltk-bible.com/cv/last_supper_cv.htm**). Alternatively, you could ask people to act out the story. Whichever method you use, invite people to reflect on how they would feel if they were the person they are focusing on.

Reflect with the group on how this was a very important time for Jesus and his disciples. Jesus knew he was going to die and wanted his best friends to have a special memory of this last meal together. Jesus also knew that his disciples were going to hurt him during the next few days, but wanted them to know he still loved them. Jesus still wants **Breaking Bread** to be a special experience when we remember him and come close to him, even though we can't see him or when we don't feel good enough for him to love us.

Share a conversation around the following questions, or others that would be helpful for your group:

1   What happened during the meal?
2   Why were these things important?
3   How do you think 'your' character felt?
4   What did Jesus say about the bread and wine that they were having for the meal?
5   What do you think he meant?
6   When you **Break Bread**, what do you think Jesus would say to you?
7   What makes, or would help to make, **Breaking Bread** special for you?

Close with a prayer: encourage people to think of something that:

- they think is amazing about God
- they would like to thank Jesus for
- they would like to tell Jesus they are sorry for or should have done better
- they want God's help for.

> Thank you, Lord, that we can remember you by sharing bread and wine together, just as you did with your special friends. We pray that **Breaking Bread** together will bring us closer to you and help us to live our lives for you. Amen

Kim's Game 👪

Put the items below on a tray. Discuss how each object relates to the story of the last supper. Then play the game: the tray is covered with a cloth and one of the items is removed. Players have to remember what has been removed and what it represents. Alternatively, you could hide the tray and ask people to remember or write down the twelve objects on it.

- a bread roll
- a cup or communion glass
- grape juice
- a picture of Da Vinci's *Last Supper* (easily printed from the internet)
- a service book
- a cross
- a bar of soap or a towel
- a jar of water (to identify the man the disciples followed before the last supper)
- a rosary, or a knot in a handkerchief (for remembrance)
- a toy cockerel, or picture of one
- a piece of paper with the word 'Sorry' written on it (to indicate the importance of repentance)
- a silver coin (to represent Jesus predicting Judas' betrayal).

Invite people to consider and discuss the following questions:

1 Which of these items is particularly special to you, and why?
2 Which of these items particularly challenges you, and why?
3 Which of these items is the least important to you, and why?

An opportunity for Godly Play 👪

You could start with the story of 'The Good Shepherd and World Communion', which encourages all ages to wonder about what the table, the bread and the wine, and the story of the last supper might mean for each of us. It asks us questions such as: Have you ever come close to this table? Where could this table really be? Have you ever come close to the bread and wine? Have you ever heard the words of the Good Shepherd? Are the people around the table happy?

You can find more on the Godly Play website (**www.godlyplay.org.uk**), or you can see a demonstration of the story on YouTube (**youtu.be/AYO_382TpCc** or search for 'The Good Shepherd and World Communion').

Messy Communion 👪

The Messy Communion resource is very useful for exploring issues around **Breaking Bread** (and specifically Holy Communion) with younger people and their families.

You can find it in Lucy Moore's book *Messy Church 2* (BRF, 2008), pp. 200–10.

Baking and breaking bread 👪 ☺

In biblical times, bread would be both baked and broken inside the home. Both take time and offer opportunities for **Fellowship**. There are many ways baking bread could be incorporated into worship.

At Northfield Methodist Church, dough made and risen prior to worship was kneaded a second time during the early part of the service and made into rolls. These were left to rise and bake during the sermon and prayers, before being brought back into the service and shared in an act of Holy Communion. The congregation found that the smell of the freshly baked rolls helped them to engage in a new way with the sacrament. Note that, for this to work, the bread rolls need to be small so that they only need a short time in the oven and there needs to be someone who is not otherwise involved in leading worship to look after the bread.

A Messy Church in Great Barr made dampers (find a recipe on the internet) and wrapped the dough around sticks. Cooking them over a fire pit was great fun and eating the slightly charred bread brought a whole new meaning to the habit of **Breaking Bread** together.

Or why not experiment with 'Bread Church' (**www.breadchurch.org.uk**)? Here each person mixes and kneads their own loaves. While the bread is rising and baking, the congregation read the Bible and share in soup together. Each person leaves with two loaves: one to eat themselves and one to give away.

FORMING THE HABIT

The ideas presented in this section are offered to help you establish or further practise **Breaking Bread** as a regular habit personally, as a church and in engagement with your local community and the wider world. You may want to consider using the ideas in more than one of these contexts.

In developing **Breaking Bread** as a regular habit, you may find some of the material in the 'Understanding the habit' section helpful too.

STORIES TO SHOW THE HABIT FORMING

How could you use these formative and transformative stories to inspire others? What stories of your own could you share?

A minister in her early years of ministry shares two stories of how **Breaking Bread** in different contexts and in different ways has been a source of blessing and a way of making Jesus known.

> I have often contested the comment that 'children should not take Communion because they don't understand what it's all about'. I confess that it makes me cross, for which adult can claim to truly understand the mystery which is Communion?
>
> I can honestly say that the most moving Communion I have shared in my ministry to date was with Messy Church on Good Friday. As we celebrated Easter together for the third time, the often boisterous gathering sat spellbound as I recounted the last week of Jesus' life; and, although we had not shared Communion before, it seemed the most natural thing in the world to pass around the bread and the cup as we sat on the floor together. I was near to tears as young children and their carers, rarely seen in church, shared in the mystery of Communion. It still moves me months later.
>
> John Wesley described Communion as a 'converting ordinance'. There is no doubt in my mind that for those gathered on that Good Friday, this very special meeting with Jesus as we broke bread in the context of Communion was a significant part of their journey of faith.
>
> On another occasion, it had been a busy day and I arrived halfway through an afternoon tea held in honour of the Queen's birthday. The event had been organised by the Holy Habits implementation team at Great Barr Methodist Church. The hall was suitably decorated in red, white and blue, and there

was a real party atmosphere as church members and invited residents of the local community ate together and enjoyed **Fellowship** with one another. I was made welcome, despite my tardiness, as they completed their quiz of all things British.

In amongst the now depleted plates of cake and evidence of strawberries and cream long gone, I spotted some broken bread. I was told how the meal had begun with grace and then bread had been broken and passed around the table as they shared together. This was no Communion table, but Jesus had been made known in the breaking of bread and the mystery of grace.

In his book *A Table for All: A challenge to church and nation*, former President of the Methodist Conferences, Inderjit Bhogal, tells the wonderful story of an occasion when he broke bread on a park bench.

> Albert is homeless. He says people call him a 'tramp' and sometimes give him money. He lives on the streets of Sheffield, where I have got to know him well. As a walker, he gave me sound advice as I prepared to walk along roads from Sheffield to London. When I saw him recently, he was sitting on a concrete bench in the city centre. He had a bandage around his head and one round his foot. 'Banged into a wall,' he said.
>
> As we got into conversation, I asked him to help me. 'I'm working on a sermon about tables and bread and parties in the wilderness,' I said. 'It seems a bit odd, but can you help me?'
>
> 'I love bread,' he said.
>
> He reached into a carrier bag beside him. His boots and walking stick were by the bag. Out of the bag he fetched bread.
>
> 'I always have bread,' he said, 'I know a shop. I turn up just before closing time. They give me a couple of loaves. With it I feed myself and my brothers and sisters who are poor.' He talked to me about all those homeless ones who walk at night as others sleep.
>
> He held out a large round cob.
>
> 'This is made from rye. I love it – my favourite,' he said. 'Try some.'
>
> He broke off a large piece with his rugged hands and held it out to me. I received it and said 'Amen' and ate it in bits over several minutes.
>
> As I ate it, he unpacked his carrier bag and brought out different kinds of bread and placed it all on the concrete slab bench, which had now become a table. Suddenly I was having a meal, and he was the host. Each loaf was held up and its contents were described. I was given a piece from each loaf.
>
> 'You need good red wine with this bread… it would be a good one for your Communion at church.'

'You need to eat this bread with cheese…'

All around us, a city centre environment with its own beauty, but a wilderness with a lifestyle of grabbing and greed and of profit before people. People racing about. Some sitting down to rest. Before me now a parable of the text: 'a table in the wilderness'.

I was being fed by one of the poorest people I know. I was a guest of honour at a table in the wilderness. 'You treat me like an honoured guest.'

The team from the Birmingham Methodist Circuit who prepared many of these **Breaking Bread** resources offered a day of creative workshops on living sacramentally, to help people from several churches explore **Breaking Bread**. Workshops included Godly Play, recycling for the Eucharist, music and the Eucharist, baking bread for the Eucharist and quiet space. The day concluded with a shared Eucharist. One participant reflected:

I didn't know what to expect when I went to the **Breaking Bread** day as part of Holy Habits. I chose to engage with some Godly Play. As the session went on and I, with others, got into the story, I was able to acknowledge that my deepest experiences of taking Communion had been in festival fields where denominational and other barriers were not present. I was able to relive the joy of **Breaking Bread** as well as within myself acknowledge the frustrations of what I felt it had sometimes been turned into within churches and the divisions that causes.

In the afternoon, after trying rosemary bread for the first time, I was able to spend some time quietly thinking, praying and writing before our final service.

During that day, God released something within me that enabled me to acknowledge the frustration that I felt, but also to set it to one side. This has freed me to engage with **Breaking Bread** more fully in a variety of situations. I have come back to focusing on the way we do Communion being secondary to Christ at the centre.

A personal reflection on inclusivity in **Breaking Bread**:

> When I was first diagnosed with a wheat intolerance, I continued to take bread at Communion as I didn't want to draw attention to myself, nor did I want to miss out on the mystery and the grace that I found at the table. I had already spent a year in Italy where I had been unable to take Communion, and I felt that I had missed out on something which I had not realised was so important to me until I was unable to receive.
>
> When I was still breastfeeding my daughter, she was diagnosed with a severe gluten intolerance, and so I stopped taking the bread. I would go and receive the wine but I felt like I no longer belonged at the table. After some time, gluten-free bread or wafers were provided for me and I felt grateful that someone was catering for my dietary needs.
>
> Then one day at the breaking of the bread, the minister took a rice cake and audibly snapped it in half. Not only that, the whole congregation were given a piece of the rice cake – of course, some moaned because it wasn't so tasty and not quite like fresh bread – but that day I felt so special, so loved, so welcome at the table.
>
> And after that I was no longer satisfied with a token gluten-free wafer or piece of bread, for on the day that the rice cake was shared by all, I felt like I was part of the body of Christ again. Perhaps I am ungrateful, but to have to go to a special place for my bread, often away from others, no longer feels like a sharing in God's grace. On the occasions when (more and more often) 'we all share in one (gluten-free) bread', God's kingdom comes and there is 'a foretaste of the heavenly banquet prepared for all people'.

PRACTICES TO HELP FORM THE HABIT

Here are some suggestions for how **Breaking Bread** can be part of a rhythm or rule of life in our personal discipleship and in and through the **Fellowship** of our churches.

Breaking Bread is more than a Holy Habit; it is a way of life, a way of being. When discussing the practice of Holy Communion at the bread-making church Somewhere Else, Barbara Glasson explained that Holy Communion is so much more than a simple shared meal or a celebratory thanksgiving of the great creating and saving acts of God. At Somewhere Else, Holy Communion was not simply something they *did*, it was what they were – a thankful, blessed, broken and sharing people.

As you explore this habit, you might like to reflect on how frequently you celebrate Holy Communion as a church.

Often (daily or weekly)

> ## Journalling
>
> Journalling is regularly reflecting on your experiences, thoughts and encounters with God and keeping a note of your reflections. See the Holy Habits Introductory Guide for more information.
>
> As you try to develop the habit of **Breaking Bread**, notice occasions when you have broken bread in different settings over the last few weeks and record them in your journal. When did you feel the presence of Jesus closely?
>
> Use your journal to record your thoughts or feelings about celebrating Holy Communion.
>
> Note down any times when you have found it difficult to celebrate Holy Communion and reflect upon why that might be.

Have you noticed the Holy Habit of **Breaking Bread** affecting your relationship with God or with others?

Daily prayer

Why not meditate daily on the line of the Lord's Prayer, 'Give us this day our daily bread', and what that means for you each coming day? How might you offer daily bread to others each day? Whenever you take a piece of bread, pause and give thanks for all that Jesus means to you.

Celebrate Holy Communion

John Wesley celebrated Holy Communion every day (note he was an Anglican priest when he did this!). Could you join with others and, observing the traditions of your church, experiment with taking Holy Communion more frequently for a shorter or longer period of time?

Sometimes (weekly or monthly)

Break bread at home

The Christian practice of **Breaking Bread** was instituted by Jesus in a home. Luke, in Acts 2:46, tells us that the first communities of Christian believers broke bread 'at home'. This simple yet sacred act can still be practised in homes today as part of a time of prayer and/or as part of a meal, simply taking and breaking bread, giving thanks for the presence and love of God in Christ and being renewed by that act in discipleship and service.

Could you instigate this practice in your home? Could you invite some friends for a meal and break bread as part of that meal? Or could you break bread with those in care homes, prisons or elsewhere?

Celebrate Holy Communion

Share Holy Communion in the church you are a part of.

Alongside this:

- Would it be helpful to share Holy Communion in different ways, either in your church or in/with other churches?
- Could you share Holy Communion together in your small group, your youth or children's group, your fresh expression of church in ways that are permitted by your particular denomination?
- Would it be helpful to share Holy Communion more often? If so, are there mid-week as well as Sunday opportunities for this? If not, how might these be provided?
- As a missional act, might you join with your minister and help others by celebrating Holy Communion in other contexts: a residential home, a prison, a school or a hospital? Many ministers, including chaplains, share Holy Communion in these contexts. Might you share with them?

Occasionally (quarterly, annually)

Celebrate Holy Communion with the wider body of Christ

Across the body of Christ there is a rich variety of ways in which the Holy Habit of **Breaking Bread** is practised. Why not spend some time exploring the ways different traditions share and live this habit and see what you learn from them? You might wish to extend this to exploring similar habits in different faith traditions.

You may wish to reflect on how accessible these other experiences are and, in the light of this, consider how open and inviting the practices in your church community are.

You might also consider exploring different forms of liturgy, such as those developed by Iona or in fresh expressions of church. A surprising amount of variation is allowed in many traditions.

Take bread to others

When you celebrate Holy Communion, do so with small bread rolls. Purchase a double quantity, and encourage each person as they take a roll for themselves to take an additional roll home to break with others – a neighbour, a family member, somebody in a local shop or a friend.

Reflect on breaking bread as a converting ordinance

John Wesley believed that Holy Communion was 'a converting ordinance'. Many fresh expressions of church are rediscovering the power that Holy Communion exerted in forming and nurturing disciples of Jesus. In a conversation recounted by Andrew Roberts, Andy Jones at Grace Church Hackney said:

> We've seen Communion act as a barometer of discipleship and as a spur to discipleship. We've seen a number of people move through the stages of watching, praying, coming forward but not partaking until they finally reach a stage of eating and drinking in faith. Similarly, we've noticed some stop eating and this has given us discipleship openings and opportunities.
>
> Andrew Roberts, *Holy Habits* (Malcolm Down Publishing, 2016), p. 147

Meanwhile, Ben Edson, who was then leading Sanctus1 in Manchester, said:

> Communion is central to Sanctus1. It is the way that people feel part of the community, and for some has been a rite of passage into the community. It helps sustain community and focus us on the central focus of our discipleship – the person of Christ.
>
> Andrew Roberts, *Holy Habits*, p. 147

How might **Breaking Bread** in the context of a service of Holy Communion help form disciples in your Christian community? What opportunities are there for people to explore this habit?

And how might the simple act of **Breaking Bread** beyond the Christian community reveal Christ's presence, as in the story of Inderjit and Albert shared earlier in the material for this Holy Habit?

QUESTIONS TO CONSIDER AS A CHURCH

These questions will help your church to consider how it can review the place of **Breaking Bread** in all of its life together. They are intended to be asked regularly rather than considered once and then forgotten. You will need to determine where in your church the responsibility for each question lies – with the whole church in a general meeting, or with the church leadership, a relevant committee or another grouping. Feel free to add more of your own.

- Can you say why **Breaking Bread** is a Holy Habit for you?
- In what ways other than Holy Communion do you, or could you, **Break Bread** to help nurture discipleship?
- How significant is it that Jesus instituted the Lord's Supper in a domestic setting, and that the Acts 2 community broke bread in their homes? In what ways could you **Break Bread** 'at home' as the believers did?
- How might **Breaking Bread** be practised as a missional act?

- What could a regular Love Feast or Agape add to the practices of your church? See the simple order of service earlier in the booklet, for example.
- Are you involved with a fresh expression of church? Is **Breaking Bread** a part of your practice? If so, what have you learnt that you might share with other churches? If not, how might it be introduced?
- Could you introduce the baking and sharing of bread as part of the life of your church, as is done at Somewhere Else in Liverpool and the House of Bread in Stafford?

Specific questions about Holy Communion

- How often do you share the sacrament of Holy Communion? Is this right for your community?
- Who might like to be involved in preparing the table, baking the bread or distributing the elements?
- How can your church be inclusive with offering bread that does not contain gluten or wine that is not alcoholic? How does this relate to worship with ecumenical friends and partners?
- Where is Holy Communion offered by your minister/chaplain in your church's name? (For example, some offer this at residential homes, others in hospitals, universities or schools.) How might you support this? Does anywhere get missed out?
- If you are a church with home groups, how could they share Holy Communion?
- How important is it to offer an open table at Holy Communion? And what does this mean for you in practice?
- Jesus said, 'Let the little children come to me' (Mark 10:14). How does this relate to the practice of **Breaking Bread**? Do children and young people in your congregation feel that they are included as equals?

CONNECTING THE HABITS

WORSHIP

BIBLICAL TEACHING

EATING TOGETHER

Breaking Bread as part of a service of Communion is a high point of Christian **Worship**.

Explore the range of Old and New Testament stories in which bread is broken, and see how this **Biblical Teaching** can greatly enrich the practice.

Breaking Bread in the context of **Eating Together** in homes was at the heart of the life of the first Christian community. How might this be relived today?

MAKING MORE DISCIPLES

As noted elsewhere, **Breaking Bread** can be a powerful evangelistic activity, making Christ known, drawing people to him and **Making More Disciples**.

THE SIMPLE, SACRED ACT OF BREAKING BREAD MAKES CHRIST KNOWN IN MANY WAYS

Breaking Bread is itself an act of **Prayer** involving thanksgiving, contrition, remembrance and renewal.

PRAYER

Breaking Bread is a prophetic symbol of brokenness and **Sharing**. We offer, we take, we break, we share.

In **Breaking Bread**, we celebrate our oneness and **Fellowship** in Christ.

FELLOWSHIP

SHARING RESOURCES

When we **Break Bread** in the context of Communion, we celebrate with **Gladness** the **Generosity** of God in the great acts of creation and salvation.

Breaking Bread in different contexts – prisons, hospitals, the homes of the housebound – is an act of true Christ-like **Serving**.

GLADNESS AND GENEROSITY

SERVING

GOING FURTHER WITH THE HABIT

DEVELOPING FURTHER PRACTICES OF BREAKING BREAD

Eucharistic living

'Eucharistic living' is not a familiar phrase for most of us. What could it mean?

It is about being open to receive the gifts of God through both the dark and light, through the creative and destructive, through the essential otherness of those who are different.

We lay ourselves open to receive the gifts of God through people of different world faith communities, different sexual orientation and different cultural backgrounds – to receive and to lay ourselves open to the possibility of transformation.

In the Eucharist, we say: God gives himself within the membranes of life and draws us into the mystery of providing within unexpected ways and unexpected places.

It is about experiencing and expressing gratitude.

Old Cyril in Notting Hill, on receiving broken bread into his outstretched hands, murmured not a pious 'amen' but a shrill 'thank you' – a thank you for God's goodness in circumstances that most of us would find it hard to bear.

Another old man, on welcoming friends into the family home, often said: 'Come and see,' and led us into the garden to look at some shrub, plant, flower or bush. He found immense joy and wonder in creation. Sometimes he even missed church on a Sunday morning and went off with his sons to a bird sanctuary and returned both exhausted and exhilarated. He said once: 'When we arrive at the gates of heaven we will be asked one question: "Have you found delight in my creation and delight in each other?"' Over and over again, he reminded us that it is God's intention that we find joy in each other.

Eucharistic living, then, is about an openness to receive that includes the possibility of transformation. It is about gratitude.

And eucharistic living is about sharing – 'The unshared remains unredeemed.'

We continue to be shaken by the sights of aid workers throwing bread into the outstretched hands of girls and boys, women and men in refugee camps, some of whom have been washed up exhausted on the shore of Greek islands. We are slow in making the connection between bread-breaking and bread-sharing.

Somewhere Else, the 'bread church' in Liverpool (**www.somewhere-else.org.uk**), continues to exist for people who don't trust the institution of the church enough to enter a conventional church building. They explore the mystery of yeast in the kneading and the rising of bread, within their own life story and also in the stories of their communities. On Tuesdays and Thursdays, people spend the day making bread and within the day they celebrate a Eucharist. The bread that they make is not for selling but for sharing, giving away in the city centre. Bread for the seller of the *Big Issue*, for Jack dying of cancer at home, for a peace vigil held for the people of East Timor, and for a Catholic priest to take home to the Presbytery. Bread for friends. Bread for bread-breaking.

Through our eucharistic living, we are drawn into 'communion', into our essential 'we-ness' in the human family, our inter-relatedness, the interconnectedness of past, present and future. And companionship? Companions are those, as the root of the word shows, who share with us the bread of life.

In our receiving, thanking and sharing, we live our 'yes' to sharing in the contrary way of Jesus.

A prayer:

> Bless, Lord, the breaking of this bread. Bless, Lord, the broken peoples of the world. Bless, Lord, them and us that we become signs of resurrection.

What happens when you can't celebrate Holy Communion?

As the material for this Holy Habit has explored, we can **Break Bread** in many different ways and contexts. At the centre of these is the practice of Holy Communion. For some, there are real practical difficulties about **Breaking Bread** in this way, with age or infirmity preventing people gathering with others as church.

Depending upon your church tradition, there are a variety of ways in which those who are housebound can partake. They include:

- Those authorised to preside at Holy Communion celebrating the sacrament in people's homes – ideally with other members of the church present to make this an act of the whole church.
- Various practices of extended Communion in which bread and wine blessed as part of a service of Holy Communion are taken out to people.

One Methodist Circuit, recognising the challenges faced by an increasing number of housebound members, decided to employ a lay pastor whose ministry was to serve those who could not leave their homes. She visited regularly, fostering a sense of **Fellowship**, and began to lead simple acts of **Worship** and **Prayer** in people's homes. As part of this, she broke bread with people through the practice of extended Communion. Those blessed by this started to tell their neighbours about the lovely lady who shared with them in this way. The neighbours asked if they could join in. And so the practice of **Breaking Bread** in the home became central to a network of missional communities. The Acts 2 picture was reborn.

Liturgy: the work of the people

Liturgy is 'the work of the people'. When it comes to **Breaking Bread** as part of Holy Communion, different groups of Christians have developed different approaches to the use of Communion liturgies. The United Reformed Church, for example, offers liturgies as resources to those presiding, but no set form of words or actions is compulsory. The Methodist Church has a range of authorised services. You may wish to explore and reflect upon the traditions, practices and liturgies of other denominations and consider how they are worshipful and nurturing. What do the different practices and liturgies have in common and what is different? Why might this be so?

The following material gives a group the opportunity to reflect on other liturgies and prepare an order of service for Holy Communion. In doing this, it will be important to consult with church leaders, inviting them to share their insights and wisdom as well as guidance on the order, traditions and practices of their particular church.

The group might brainstorm the common or essential components of a service of Holy Communion – putting ideas on a flipchart and then putting them into order. It is important that the liturgy is consistent, so beware a pick'n'mix approach, which risks confusing metaphors.

Reference might then be made to a typical structure, such as this outline – or, depending on your group, the 'classical order' – which includes the fourfold action of taking, blessing, breaking and sharing:

- invitation
- narrative of the institution
- prayer of thanksgiving
- the breaking of the bread and pouring of the wine
- the sharing of bread and wine
- prayer after Holy Communion.

Often included are:

- an offertory
- seasonal and proper prefaces
- the peace
- other prayers, particularly the Lord's Prayer.

The common pattern outlined above has been shaped over many years, so any reworking needs to be very carefully thought through, honouring the tradition as well as being open to the movement of the Spirit.

Sharing your story

Stories of **Breaking Bread** can be particularly precious and personal, in the beauty and mystery of what it means to us on our faith journey. Emotions and opinions around **Breaking Bread** may differ greatly, but 'it's good to talk' and we should take care to listen respectfully.

How about having a regular slot at Holy Communion services and inviting individuals (of all ages and life stages) to share what Holy Communion means to them?

Or perhaps you could invite people, as part of a discursive Ministry of the Word, to consider what **Breaking Bread** means in daily life when we're not sharing in a formal act of Holy Communion.

Perhaps you could invite ecumenical friends to share what **Breaking Bread** means to them, and then break bread together (being careful to honour different traditions).

ARTS AND MEDIA

There are many films and books containing scenes about **Breaking Bread** which could be used as an illustration in worship. However, it is suggested that the following films and books are watched or read in their entirety and followed by a discussion to go deeper into the topic of **Breaking Bread**.

Films

Cast Away (12, 2000, 2h23m)

In *Cast Away*, the struggle to survive and the scarcity of food mean that, on the castaway's return to civilisation, the emotional significance of various things including food is very noticeable. At one stage, Tom Hanks appears to try to share food with an inanimate object. This film is useful for discussion of symbolism and of attaching of value to an item.

- This film illustrates the overlapping of **Eating Together** and **Breaking Bread**. Is there something sacramental about the castaway's desire to share food with an inanimate object?
- How does this challenge our understanding of **Breaking Bread** and its relationship to **Eating Together**?

Of Gods and Men (15, 2010, 2h2m)

A monastic community stay in Algeria, even though they know it may cost them their lives. Their life is prayer. (French with English subtitles.)

- What part does **Breaking Bread** play in sustaining the monks in faithful discipleship?
- How does the monks' extreme situation speak to your context?

👪 The Miracle Maker (U, 2000, 1h30m)

An animated film of the life and teaching of Jesus, which features several episodes of **Breaking Bread**, including the feeding of the 5,000 and the last supper. This is an excellent resource for introducing the last supper to children and younger people in particular. For others, you may wish to discuss:

- What significance is there in Jesus **Breaking Bread** with his disciples in a domestic setting?

Places in the Heart (PG, 1984, 1h51m)

A US Depression-era Texan widow tries to save a family farm with the help of a blind white man and a poor black man. An extraordinary community is formed.

- In the final scene, bread is broken and shared as part of a Holy Communion service. How does the broken bread feed them?
- What can we learn from this film about Communion and community?

Books: fiction

Are there people in your church or local community who would like to discuss some of these books at a book club? Guidance on how to form these is widely available online, and you could also ask denominational training officers for help.

👨‍👩‍👧 Hillytown Biscuit Church and the Custard Cream Communion Club
Ruth Whiter (Christian Education Publications, 2010)

As new children join the church, they explore how to live together.

- Read the final chapter: do the preceding chapters make the service of Holy Communion more or less significant?
- How does the book help you to understand the importance of **Breaking Bread** together in all-age groups?

👨‍👩‍👧 Making Heart-Bread
Matthew Linn, Sheila Fabricant Linn and Dennis Linn (Paulist Press, 2006)

This book presents a spiritual practice of making heart-bread to add richness and meaning to daily life.

- Could you use this practice alongside the petition in the Lord's Prayer for daily bread?

The Power and the Glory
Graham Greene (Vintage Classics, 1940)

The moving story of a priest who, though deeply anxious that he has been a failure, continues to administer the Mass at a time and in a place where the practice has been banned.

- How might the divine simplicity of **Breaking Bread** be subversive in a kingdom way?

👨‍👩‍👧 The Velveteen Rabbit
Margery Williams, illustrated by William Nicholson (George H. Doran Company, 1922)

The story of a stuffed rabbit who is on a mission to become real, or known, through the love of his owner.

- How do we discover the reality of Christ's presence in the act of **Breaking Bread**?

Books: non-fiction

An Altar in the World: Finding the sacred beneath our feet
Barbara Brown Taylor (Canterbury Press Norwich, 2009)

A book that takes a broad view of the sacramental, finding symbols of grace in the world around.

- How might we see more sacred signs of grace in the midst of life?
- What does the beauty and the simplicity of **Breaking Bread** say to us about the sacred?

Bread in Our Hands: Feeding God's people in hungry times
Julie M. Hulme (Inspire, 2008)

A detailed exploration of the feeding of the 5,000 and what that story has to teach us about faith.

- Use this book individually or as a group to explore what the story of the feeding of the 5,000 has to teach us about **Breaking Bread** together.

👥 Hey, God, What Is Communion?
Roxie Cawood Gibson (Jim Gibson, 2005)

A delightful conversation between a young child and God, exploring the meaning of Holy Communion.

Read this book to an all-age congregation and see what questions and comments emerge as you explore the meaning of Holy Communion together.

His Presence Makes the Feast: Holy Communion in the Methodist Church and Share This Feast: Reflecting on Holy Communion
(Methodist Publishing House, 2003/2006)

These two very helpful, visually stunning resources explore the nurturing and transforming power of the practice of **Breaking Bread** in the context of Holy Communion.

- How might you use these books to foster conversation around the ways in which you celebrate the Lord's Supper?

The One Loaf: An everyday celebration
Joy Mead (Wild Goose Publications, 2004)

A book which explores the making and the mystery of bread – growing, making, baking, sharing – in story and recipe, poetry and prayer.

- The book claims that to take and eat means to take and live – that to share bread is to share our life. Do you agree? And if so, how could this be more fully realised?

Other Communions of Jesus: Eating and drinking the good news way
John Henson (O Books, 2006)

Henson suggests that, by basing our practice and understanding of Holy Communion on the last supper, we have ignored those other occasions when Jesus ate and drank with people, and have unwittingly limited our practices of **Breaking Bread**.

- What might we learn from the other occasions when Jesus ate with others and broke bread?

A Table for All: A challenge to church and nation
Inderjit Bhogal (Penistone Publications, 2000)

A prophetic challenge to the practices of **Breaking Bread** and Holy Communion, and how they can be experiences of radical hospitality, justice and change.

- How can **Breaking Bread** be a prophetic as well as a pastoral act? What does this mean for your practices of **Breaking Bread**?

Articles and online media

Good News Stories

- House of Bread (**youtu.be/ ojw2cHXQpbU** or search YouTube for 'Good News Stories with Nick'). This story is also listed in **Eating Together**.

Imagining Abundance

Search Julie Hulme's site, Imagining Abundance (**www. imaginingabundance.co.uk**), for 'Living Bread', for a fantastic series of reflections and questions around the theme of living bread (**www. imaginingabundance.co.uk/ the-prospect-of-a-feast/living-bread. html**).

Music

The following musical item may help you to explore and reflect further on this habit.

Breaking Bread
Paul Field

A musical backdrop that can be used with Holy Communion liturgy. Songbook with dance and drama (Kingsway Publications, 1988). Could you use some of this material to enhance your services of Holy Communion?

Poetry

A number of poems are presented or referenced below. Choose one to reflect on.

You may wish to consider some of the following questions:

- What does this poem say to you about **Breaking Bread**?
- Which images do you find helpful or unhelpful?
- How is your practice of **Breaking Bread** challenged by this poem?
- Could you write a poem to share with others the virtues of **Breaking Bread**?

Offering

Consider a child's painting:
By most objective standards, it is not good art,
But when placed proudly in the parent's hands,
It has tremendous worth, delighting the heart,
If not always the eye.
Gentle questioning will be required
To establish what the picture represents,
And which way up it should be hung,
And the answers will become part of the wonder,
Recalled each time the adult eye lingers
Over the work,
Now mounted on some kitchen cupboard,
Or fridge door.
In the moment of giving and receiving,
Which is the lover, which the beloved?
The child's glad offering,
And the adult's glad receiving,
Are each their own counterpart,
In a story of love,
Given and received, received and given.

Tony McClelland

Breaking Bread – Simply?

People, animals, hopes, dreams, despair
mingling in the field.
They are together here and now.
Friends and strangers gathering
around simple bread and wine.

The bread might be white or brown,
Handmade or processed, gluten free or gluten full.
Some mutter it matters,
perhaps wafers would be better.
There is a sigh as people gather,
so much for simple bread and wine.
The wine sits in a simple beaker,
rich and red it flows.
Then the muttering begins again.
Chalice or small cup?
So much for simple bread and wine.

A book is opened, words recited,
passed down from age to age.
There is a profound silence for a moment
as their power is absorbed.
But then the muttering begins again
about how to interpret meaning.
So much for simple bread and wine.

Then it's time to share this Godly supper.
Making sure all can share together
in this unifying experience.
But the muttering is growing louder
About who should serve and who should eat.
So much for simple bread and wine.

Then a shepherd enters the scene,
holding a small child by the hand.
They sit and smile at each other
as he sits and breaks a piece of bread.
Handing it over saying have eat,
Remember me next time you simply eat.

The wine sits in the beaker,
the child's mother looks worried.
The shepherd smiles and picks up some cherryade.
He hands it to the child,
Saying something is going to happen to me
but through it you shall live.
Remember me next time you simply drink.

Sally Rush, sallyrush.blogspot.co.uk/2016/02/holy-habit-breaking-bread-simply.html

Devotions 28: Place of Grace, Saints Dance
Ian Adams, from *Unfurling* (Canterbury Press, 2015)

The Vast Ocean Begins Just Outside Our Church: The Eucharist
Mary Oliver, from *Thirst* (Bloodaxe Books, 2007)

Mass for Hard Times
R.S. Thomas, from *Later Collected Poems 1998–2000*
(Bloodaxe Books, 2004)

The Dalit Madonna

Jyoti Sahi (b. 1944): oil on canvas, c. 2002, 148 x 119 cm.

From the Methodist Modern Art Collection, © TMCP, used with permission.

You can download this image from: www.methodist.org.uk/artcollection

This is a large and striking image of a Madonna and Child. The artist, born in India, has spoken about his choice of title and composition, which draw on local cultural traditions, some Christian, some from other faiths and folklore. The folk symbol of the grinding stone is intrinsic to the painting. It consists of a fixed and stable 'Mother Stone' into which fits a smaller 'Baby Stone'. The Baby Stone is free to move about and is used to grind foodstuffs which are placed in the hollow of the Mother Stone.

- Reflect on the title of the painting and the meaning of the word 'Dalit', which means 'broken'. What is the significance of a Dalit woman in the role of Mary?
- Do the shapes in the folds of the garment remind you of any elements of the natural world? What does the painting say to you about Christ's provision?
- Ignatius of Antioch, an early father of the church, said, 'There can be no bread without a process of breaking and transforming.' Do you find this a hopeful painting?
- What feelings does **Breaking Bread** evoke in you? Can you paint or draw them?

Freshly baked

Bread is broken and blessed; thanksgiving is offered; bread is shared. In what ways is this an ordinary, everyday action? What makes it special? How might the breaking of bread be a source of blessing? How does this picture speak to you?

Credits

Contributions to this booklet came from: Caroline Homan (lead Birmingham Circuit Editor), Fiona Barker, Andrew Brazier, Ben Clymo, Jessica Dalton Cheetham, Donald Eadie, Dorothy Graham, Caz Hague, Jean Hamilton, Deborah Humphries, Jill James, Tony McClelland, Sarah Middleton, Tom Milton, Tricia Mitchell, Tony Moodie, Helen Pollard, Meg Prowting, Andrew Roberts, Sally Rush, Stuart Scott, Karen Webber and Frances Young.

'This set of ten resources will enable churches and individuals to begin to establish "habits of faithfulness". In the United Reformed Church, we are calling this process of developing discipleship, "Walking the Way: Living the life of Jesus today" and I have no doubt that this comprehensive set of resources will enable us to do just that.'

Revd Richard Church, Deputy General Secretary (Discipleship), United Reformed Church

'Here are some varied and rich resources to help further deepen our discipleship of Christ, encouraging and enabling us to adopt the life-transforming habits that make for following Jesus.'

Revd Dr Martyn Atkins, Team Leader & Superintendent Minister, Methodist Central Hall, Westminster

'The Holy Habits resources will help you, your church, your fellowship group, to engage in a journey of discovery about what it really means to be a disciple today. I know you will be encouraged, challenged and inspired as you read and work your way through each chapter. There is lots to study together and pray about, and that can only be good as our churches today seek to bring about the kingdom of God.'

Revd Loraine Mellor, President of the Methodist Conference 2017/18

'The Holy Habits resources help weave the spiritual through everyday life. They're a great tool that just get better with use. They help us grow in our desire to follow Jesus as their concern is formation not simply information.'

Olive Fleming Drane and John Drane

'The Holy Habits resources are an insightful and comprehensive manual for living in the way of Jesus in the 21st century: an imaginative, faithful and practical gift for the church that will sustain and invigorate our life and mission in a demanding world. The Holy Habits resources are potentially transformational for a church.'

Revd Ian Adams, Mission Spirituality Adviser for Church Mission Society

'To understand the disciplines of the Christian life without practising them habitually is like owning a fine collection of soap but never having a wash. The team behind Holy Habits knows this, which is why they have produced these excellent and practical resources. Use them, and by God's grace you will grow in holiness.'

Paul Bayes, Bishop of Liverpool

'The Holy Habits resources are a rich mine of activities for all ages to help change minds, attitudes and behaviours. I love the way many different people groups are represented and celebrated, and the constant references to the complex realities of 21st-century life.'

Lucy Moore, Founder of BRF's Messy Church